Do-It-Yourself

CREATIVE

WRITING

JOURNAL

Write Your Own Story

Color, Draw & Doodle

The Thinking Tree Publishing Company, LLC

My Stories

Name:

Date & Age:

Address:

Write a short Story to Go with the Picture.

Title: _____   Date: _____

Write a short Story to Go with the Picture.

Title: _____   Date: _____

Write a short Story to Go with the Picture.

Title: _____   Date: _____

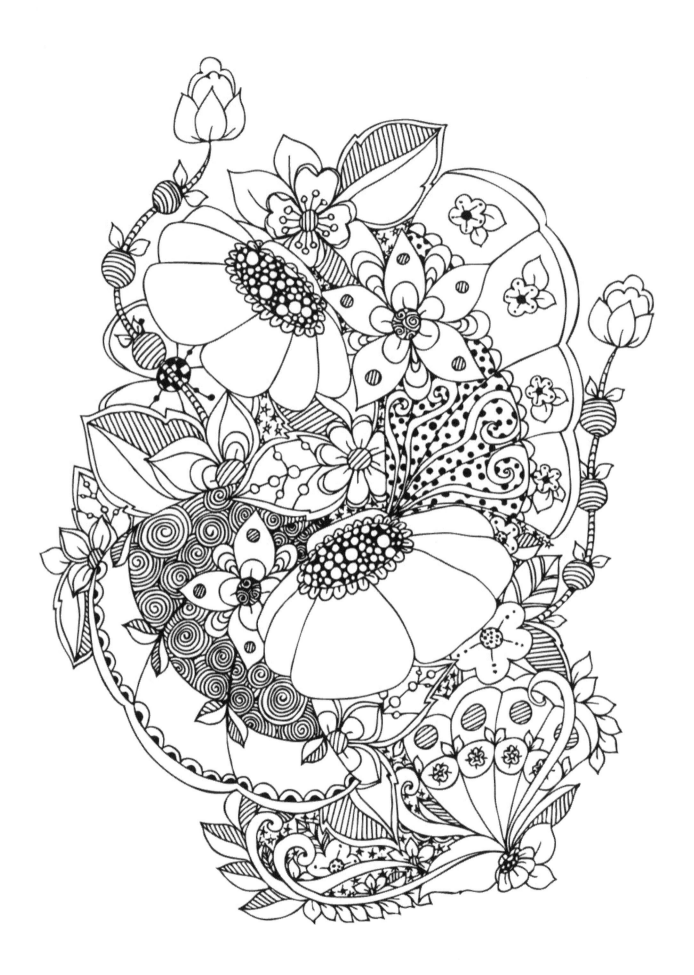

Write a short Story to Go with the Picture.

Title: _____   Date: _____

Write a short Story to Go with the Picture.

Title: _____ Date: _____

Write a short Story to Go with the Picture.

Title: _____   Date: _____

Write a short Story to Go with the Picture.

Title: _____   Date: _____

_____

_____

_____

_____

_____

_____

_____

_____

_____

_____

_____

_____

_____

Write a short Story to Go with the Picture.

Title: _____   Date: _____

Write a short Story to Go with the Picture.

Title: _____   Date: _____

Write a short Story to Go with the Picture.

Title: _____   Date: _____

Write a short Story to Go with the Picture.

Title: _____   Date: _____

_____
_____
_____
_____
_____
_____
_____
_____
_____
_____
_____
_____
_____
_____
_____

Write a short Story to Go with the Picture.

Title: _____   Date: _____

Write a short Story to Go with the Picture.

Title: _____   Date: _____

_____

_____

_____

_____

_____

_____

_____

_____

_____

_____

_____

_____

_____

Write a short Story to Go with the Picture.

Title: _____   Date: _____

Write a short Story to Go with the Picture.

Title: _____ Date: _____

Write a short Story to Go with the Picture.

Title: _____   Date: _____

Write a short Story to Go with the Picture.

Title: _____   Date: _____

Write a short Story to Go with the Picture.

Title: _____ Date: _____

Write a short Story to Go with the Picture.

Title: _____   Date: _____

Write a short Story to Go with the Picture.

Title: _____   Date: _____

Write a short Story to Go with the Picture.

Title: _____ Date: _____

Write a short Story to Go with the Picture.

Title: _____ Date: _____

Write a short Story to Go with the Picture.

Title: _____   Date: _____

Write a Short Story & Draw a Picture.

Title: _____   Date: _____

Write a Short Story & Draw a Picture.

Title: _____   Date: _____

Write a Short Story & Draw a Picture.

Title: _____   Date: _____

Write a Short Story & Draw a Picture.

Title: _____ Date: _____

Write a Short Story & Draw a Picture.

Title: _____ Date: _____

Write a Short Story & Draw a Picture.

Title: _____   Date: _____

Write a Short Story & Draw a Picture.

Title: _____ Date: _____

Write a Short Story & Draw a Picture.

Title: _____   Date: _____

Write a Short Story & Draw a Picture.

Title: _____ Date: _____

Write a Short Story & Draw a Picture.

Title: _____ Date: _____

Write a Short Story & Draw a Picture.

Title: _____ Date: _____

Write a Short Story & Draw a Picture.

Title: _____   Date: _____

Write a Short Story & Draw a Picture.

Title: _____ Date: _____

Write a Short Story & Draw a Picture.

Title: _____   Date: _____

_____

_____

_____

_____

_____

_____

_____

_____

_____

_____

_____

_____

_____

_____

Write a Short Story & Draw a Picture.

Title: _____   Date: _____

Write a Short Story & Draw a Picture.

Title: _____ Date: _____

Write a Short Story & Draw a Picture.

Title: _____ Date: _____

Write a Short Story & Draw a Picture.

Title: _____ Date: _____

Write a Short Story & Draw a Picture.

Title: _____   Date: _____

Write a Short Story & Draw a Picture.

Title: _____   Date: _____

Write a Short Story & Draw a Picture.

Title: _____   Date: _____

_____

_____

_____

_____

_____

_____

_____

_____

_____

_____

_____

_____

Write a Short Story & Draw a Picture.

Title: _____   Date: _____

Write a Short Story & Draw a Picture.

Title: _____ Date: _____

Write a Short Story & Draw a Picture.

Title: _____   Date: _____

_____

_____

_____

_____

_____

_____

_____

_____

_____

_____

_____

_____

Made in the USA
Lexington, KY
07 May 2016